HOPE AND HER DILEMMAS

HER SIDE OF STORY

D. V. AURORA

ISBN 979-888569187-1

To my love

Contents

Preface   *vii*

1. I Love You   1

2. Dreams   4

3. One Sided Love   5

4. Wishes   6

5. Be Yourself   7

6. Little Girl   8

7. Finding Her Way   9

8. Brave   10

9. What Is Love   11

10. Felt Alive   12

11. You Deserve Better   13

Preface

About the overwhelming thoughts

and different emotions

we feel

sometimes confused about

what is right or wrong

1. I LOVE YOU

I love you
your morning face
when i try to wake u up
and u still want to sleep
a little more
I love you
when u pull me in the blanket
and hug tightly
don't want to let go
I love you
when you kiss me
while in sleep
and when you put your leg
right over me
not letting me slip away
keeping me warm
in those chilled nights
and refusing to take your hand
off my back
I love you
how u like me
to run my fingers

over your back
and pin my nails
into your cheeks
I love you
when you want to kiss me again
just after we kissed
and as soon as i get home
to you
I love you
when you make me omelette
with i love you scribbled on it
with a smile :)
I love you
when you help me
getting dressed
after we made out
or sometimes
how u want to sleep naked
doing nothing
I love you
when you dont want me to know
that you are hurt
and try to hide it under
your fake smile
and all you want to do
is bury your head
in my stomach

wrap around quietly
and sleep
I love you
when you pull me closer
with your hand
on my waist
to pose for a photograph
or when you pout
for a selfie with me
I love you

2. DREAMS

With her hope for dreams
that they will come true one day
With a smile on the face
she is walking on her way
Never let her distract from the path
the only thing to God she prays
The goal she wants to achieve
is still far away
A lot of situations
In which she has to Stay
Facing them with courage
not letting herself to stray
Step by step, will reach her goal
with God's blessings and parent's pray.

3. ONE SIDED LOVE

Never have she loved someone
as much as she loves him
and even though he hurts her
her feelings will remian true
Holding her tight
he comes into her dreams
which she knows
might never real seem.
Why havn't she told him
and never did he realize
that she love him
unconditionally and crazy like
Doesn't he ever feel
like she does for him
never has he noticed
that she really loves him.

4. WISHES

Free from all the chains
she wanna fly
on high heights
in the sky
That day will come
will definately come
when she will achieve all she wants
and then no one will say anything
just they can't
She wants her wishes to come true
don't wanna make them pie in the sky
that day will come
when she will walk high

5. BE YOURSELF

Never let anyone rule you
be the only master of your life
Do whatever you want
don't bother about the strife
People just need something to talk
all these things are rife

6. LITTLE GIRL

A girl with open mind
by heart she is very kind.
She is like a kid
never worries about what she did
With an Innocent smile on her face
when meets she always embrace
Never mind what people say
keep going on her way
The way She speak
is very sweet and unique
Be happy is her common quote
for us is a pleasure note

7. FINDING HER WAY

Searching for an answer
trying to find the way
where the life is going
what is it trying to say
New wishes new dreams
on every new day
and also some old ones,
which she has
to make them true
she will surely find a way.

8. BRAVE

With all the heartbreaks
and all the pain
she has been through
Still not afraid to love
Holding on to the thought
that she ll find her true love
the one she always dreamt of
The love that will not hurt
that will not end in heartbreak
that will last forever and beyond
The love that she always wanted
she will find the one

9. WHAT IS LOVE

What is love
she often asks herself
Is it when we feel attracted to a stranger
the stranger who helped us out of nowhere
Is it when we hold hands
rr when they are wrapped in each others arms
when he cooks for her the dinner
when he picks her up
and slides into the blanket on a cold day
or when he takes her out
On a romantic date

10. FELT ALIVE

What is the point of living
if you have never experienced the love
or compassion and empathy
Have you ever looked at someone
and it felt like world to you
Have you ever held an infant
who looks at you and smiles
Have you ever looked at the sky
and felt limitless
Have you looked at the never ending waters
of the sea and wander
what resides on the other end
Have you ever helped someone
knowing they can never help you
Have you ever felt alive?

11. YOU DESERVE BETTER

you deserve better, lovey
he said
be better then
for me, for us
she said
irony of love
he loves you
and yet cant change
his behaviour for you
knowing all this while
what he is doing
is not what she deserves
wishes a better world for her
and yet cant put any effort
to provide the same
confused what to believe
his sincere words
or his lack of effort
hoping he will improve
and match his words

to make a better world
for both of them
she continues
broken heart
everytime disappointed
not seeing him try
how careless one can be
to make big promises
only to break all one day
you deserve better, lovey
he said
nothing new
nothing that i already didn't know
yet it hit differently
that day
when i was trying to talk
and he was busy
as usual
in his own world
Which had no place
for me now
or never had maybe
i realised
how we keep
compromising and forgiving
the ones we love
until we get tired

of forgiving them
and finally unlove
fall out of love
the same love we once thought
we can't live without

www.ingramcontent.com/pod-product-compliance
Lightning Source LLC
Chambersburg PA
CBHW020948160726
47993CB00007B/3000